Cambridge Young Lear
English Tests

Cambridge
Movers 5

Examination papers from

University of Cambridge
ESOL Examinations:

English for Speakers of Other Languages

CAMBRIDGE
UNIVERSITY PRESS

CU00546279

CAMBRIDGE UNIVERSITY PRESS
Cambridge, New York, Melbourne, Madrid, Cape Town,
Singapore, São Paulo, Delhi, Tokyo, Mexico City

Cambridge University Press
The Edinburgh Building, Cambridge CB2 8RU, UK

www.cambridge.org
Information on this title: www.cambridge.org/9780521693288

© Cambridge University Press 2007

This publication is in copyright. Subject to statutory exception
and to the provisions of relevant collective licensing agreements,
no reproduction of any part may take place without the written
permission of Cambridge University Press.

First published 2007
6th printing 2011

Printed in the United Kingdom at the University Press, Cambridge

A catalogue record for this publication is available from the British Library

ISBN 978-0-521-69328-8 Student's Book
ISBN 978-0-521-69329-5 Answer Booklet
ISBN 978-0-521-69330-1 Audio Cassette
ISBN 978-0-521-69331-8 Audio CD

Cambridge University Press has no responsibility for the persistence or
accuracy of URLs for external or third-party internet websites referred to in
this publication, and does not guarantee that any content on such websites is,
or will remain, accurate or appropriate. Information regarding prices, travel
timetables and other factual information given in this work is correct at
the time of first printing but Cambridge University Press does not guarantee
the accuracy of such information thereafter.

Cover design by David Lawton
Produced by HL Studios

Contents

Part 1
– 5 questions –

Listen and draw lines. There is one example.

Jane   Nick   Tom   Sally

Bill   Sue   Sam

Part 2
– 5 questions –

Listen and write. There is one example.

	Please look for:	Sports bag
1	Name of child:	Daisy ....
2	Colour of bag:	....
3	The bag was:	next to ....
4	Inside the bag was:	a ....
5	Child's address:	.... Top Street

Part 3
– 5 questions –

What did Paul do last week?
Listen and draw a line from the day to the correct picture. There is one example.

Part 4
– 5 questions –

Listen and tick (✔) the box. There is one example.

What does the girl want to buy?

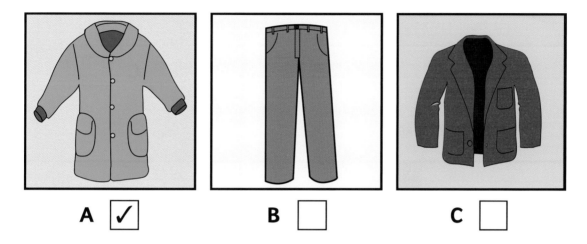

A ✓   B ☐   C ☐

1   What did the boy draw?

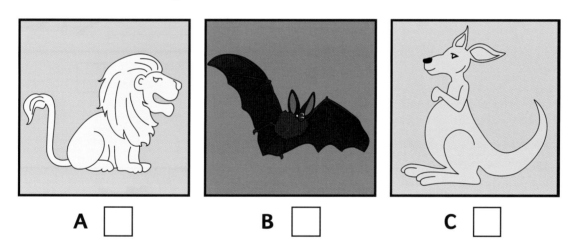

A ☐   B ☐   C ☐

2   Where can they have the picnic?

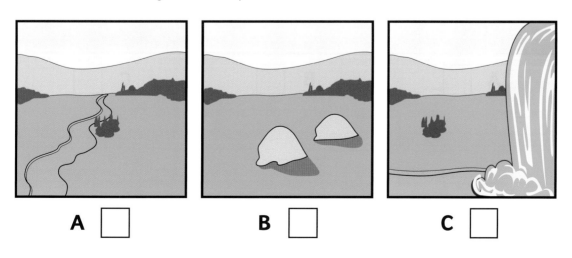

A ☐   B ☐   C ☐

3   What's the parrot doing?

4   Where's the blanket?

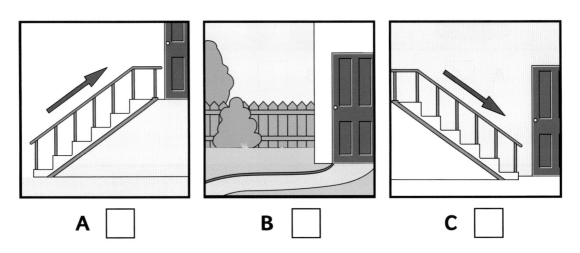

5   Which girl is Ann's sister?

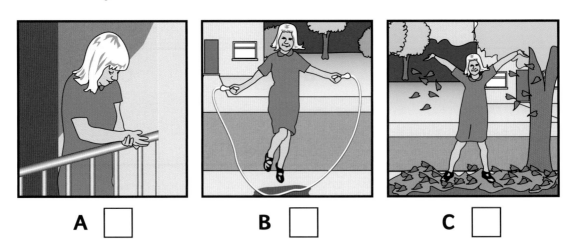

Part 5
– 5 questions –

Listen and colour and draw. There is one example.

Reading and Writing

Part 1
– 6 questions –

Look and read. Choose the correct words and write them on the lines. There is one example.

fruit

a market

a library

a picnic

a café

a lift

pasta

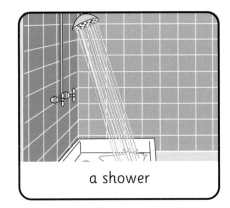

a shower

Example

People go to this place to drink, eat, and
talk to their friends.   ....*a café*...........

Questions

1   You wash your body and your hair in this.   ....

2   You sit and eat in a field or on a beach for this.   ....

3   You can buy food and clothes here.   ....

4   You go up or down between floors in this.   ....

5   Apples, bananas, lemons and oranges are
    examples of this.   ....

6   You can read books here or take them
    home to read.   ....

Part 2
– 6 questions –

Look and read. Write yes or no.

Examples

A pirate is sitting on a box.   *yes*

There are six hippos in the picture.   *no*

Questions

1   The girls are playing a game of badminton.

....

2   There is a green and yellow parrot on the boy's shoulder.

....

3   A big brown monkey is climbing a mountain.

....

4   A woman with a red skirt has got a bowl of pineapples.

....

5   There is a big snake in the tree above the crocodile.

....

6   A man and a woman are crossing the river in a boat.

....

Part 3
– 6 questions –

Read the text and choose the best answer.

Example

Nick:	Hello, Jane.
Jane:	(A) Hello, Nick.
	B Goodbye, Nick.
	C Thank you, Nick.

Questions

1	**Nick:**	Where did you go at the weekend?
	Jane:	A I go to see Kim in her new house.
		B I went to see Kim in her new house.
		C I can see Kim in her new house.

2 **Nick:**   Where does she live now?

   Jane: A   In your house.
                B   In the lake.
                C   In a village.

3 **Nick:**   Does she like her new home?

   Jane: A   Yes, we did.
                B   Yes, she does.
                C   Yes, you do.

4 **Nick:**   How's her brother, Ben?

   Jane: A   He's fine.
                B   He's tall with brown hair.
                C   He's eight.

5 **Nick:**   What did you do with Kim on Saturday?

   Jane: A   You sailed a boat with her.
                B   She went fishing with you.
                C   We swam in the sea.

6 **Nick:**   Great! Can I go with you to see Kim and Ben one day?

   Jane: A   OK.
                B   So do I.
                C   Yes, I can.

Part 4

– 7 questions –

Read the story. Choose a word from the box. Write the correct word next to numbers 1–6. There is one example.

Sally and her family lived on a farm. They had a lot of animals: sheep,

..........cows.........., goats, chickens and horses. Every morning before

school, Sally went to see her grey horse, 'Cloud'. She gave him some

(1) .... to eat for his breakfast and talked to him. Then

she said goodbye. But last Friday, she didn't **(2)** ....

Cloud's door carefully when she went to see him.

Sally went to school in Dad's **(3)** .... In class that

morning, the teacher drew a horse on the **(4)** .... 'Now

you draw one!' he said. Sally started to draw Cloud. Then she looked out of

the **(5)** .... There was Cloud! 'Look children,' said the

teacher. 'There's a horse in the playground. You can draw it.'

'That's MY horse!' said Sally. The children laughed. After the class, Sally

(6) .... home on Cloud.

Example

(7) **Now choose the best name for the story.**

Tick one box.

Cloud goes to school	☐
Cloud has a lesson	☐
The teacher draws Cloud	☐

Part 5

– 10 questions –

Look at the pictures and read the story. Write words to complete the sentences about the story. You can use 1, 2 or 3 words.

Jim's Birthday

On Sunday, Jim went to the mountains with his parents. In the afternoon, it snowed. At home that evening, Jim wasn't very well. 'You've got a temperature, Jim,' his mum said. 'Have some soup and then go to bed.' But he didn't want any soup. He wasn't hungry.

Examples

Jim and his parents went to ......the mountains...... on Sunday.

On Sunday afternoon, it ......snowed...... .

Questions

1   Jim had a .... on Sunday evening.

2   Jim didn't have .... because he wasn't hungry.

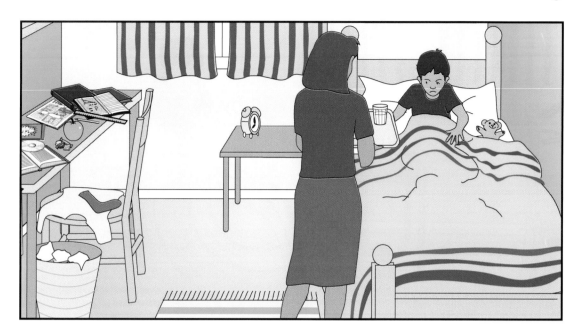

Jim slept all night, but he wasn't better in the morning. He didn't go to school that day. He was too ill and he slept all day. He got up in the evening and watched television. His mum gave him some chicken and rice, but he wasn't hungry. He only ate some rice and drank some milk. He went to bed, but he wasn't tired. He didn't sleep very well. He woke up in the night and read his book.

3   In the morning, ... wasn't better.

4   Jim couldn't go to .... that day because he was too ill.

5   The only thing that Jim ate was ....

6   When Jim woke up that night, he ....

In the morning, Jim was sad. 'Today's my birthday,' he thought, 'but I can't go to school and see my friends.' But Jim's mum and dad gave him a great present – a new computer. He was very happy because he loved computer games. Then some of his friends from school came to see him. 'Happy Birthday!' they said. 'This is for you, too!' It was Jim's favourite DVD! On Wednesday, he went back to school because he was better again.

7   Jim's parents gave him a .... for his birthday.

8   Some of Jim's .... went to see him.

9   Jim's second present was ....

10   Jim went back to school on .... when he was better.

Blank Page

Part 6

– 5 questions –

Read the text. Choose the right words and write them on the lines.

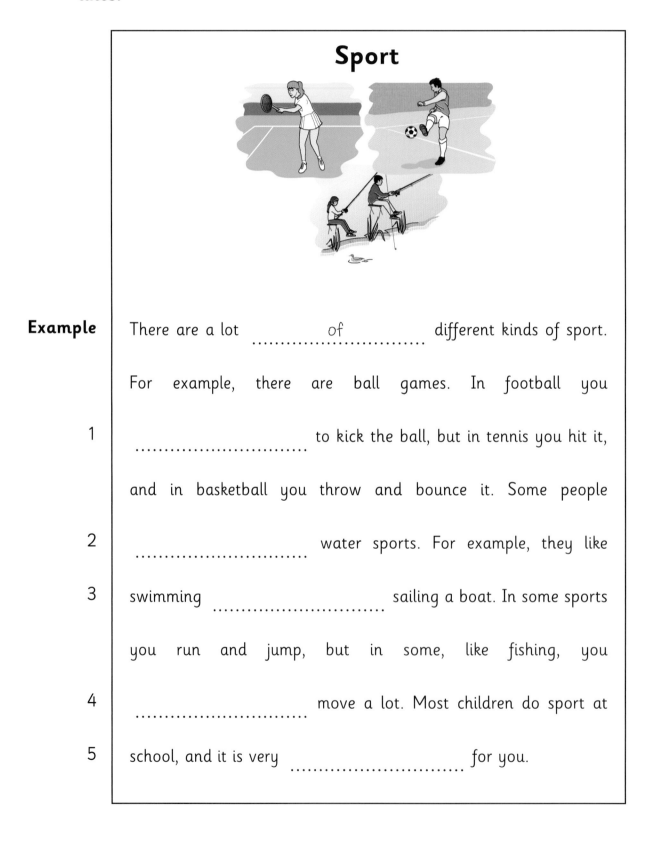

Sport

Example   There are a lot .... of .... different kinds of sport.

For example, there are ball games. In football you

1   .... to kick the ball, but in tennis you hit it,

and in basketball you throw and bounce it. Some people

2   .... water sports. For example, they like

3   swimming .... sailing a boat. In some sports

you run and jump, but in some, like fishing, you

4   .... move a lot. Most children do sport at

5   school, and it is very .... for you.

Example	with	for	of
1	has	have	had
2	enjoys	enjoy	enjoying
3	or	because	than
4	doesn't	didn't	don't
5	good	better	best

Part 1
– 5 questions –

Listen and draw lines. There is one example.

Mary   Bill   Nick   Sally

Jill   Peter   John

Part 2
– 5 questions –

Listen and write. There is one example.

Things to do today

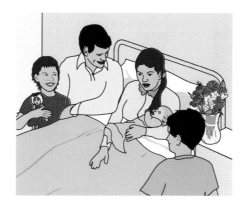

At supermarket

Buy: .... *a video* ....

1   a new ....

2   and ....

3 **Then go to:**   ....

At hospital

4   Mum needs: four ....

5   and her ....

Part 3
– 5 questions –

What did Nick do last week?
Listen and draw a line from the day to the correct picture. There is one example.

Monday

Tuesday

Wednesday

Thursday

Friday

Saturday

Sunday

Part 4
– 5 questions –

Listen and tick (✔) the box. There is one example.

What does the man want to buy?

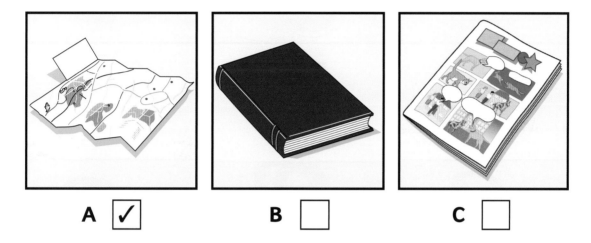

A ✔   B ☐   C ☐

1   What did the boy wash?

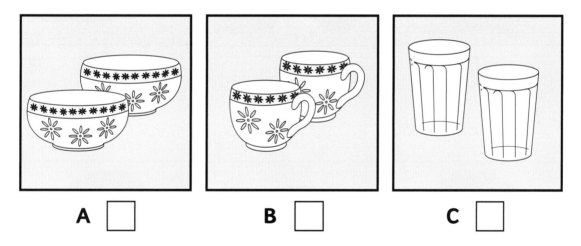

A ☐   B ☐   C ☐

2   What did Sue buy?

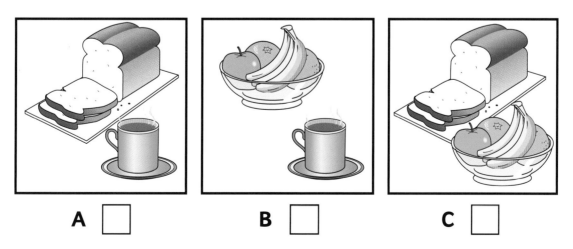

A ☐   B ☐   C ☐

3   What's the baby doing?

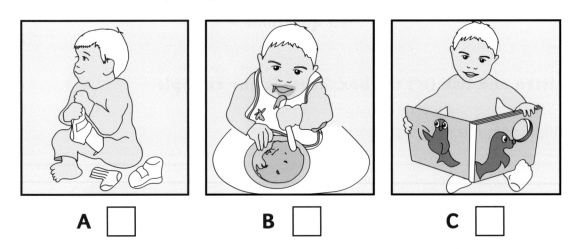

A ☐   B ☐   C ☐

4   Where's the cheese?

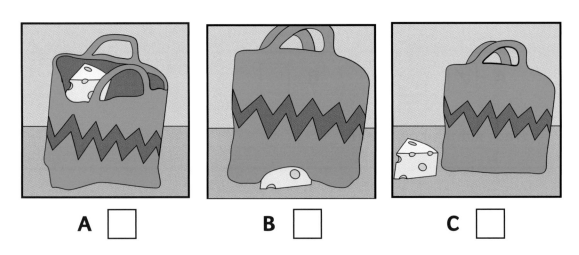

A ☐   B ☐   C ☐

5   Which child is Jim?

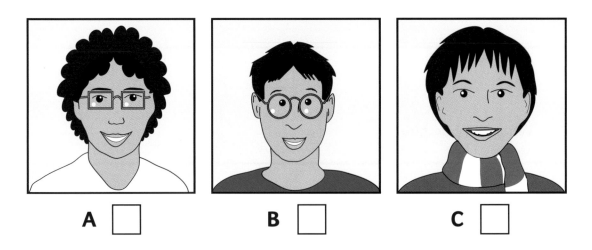

A ☐   B ☐   C ☐

Part 5
– 5 questions –

Listen and colour and draw. There is one example.

Reading and Writing

Part 1
– 6 questions –

Look and read. Choose the correct words and write them on the lines. There is one example.

a jungle

mountains

a rainbow

stars

the sea

a waterfall

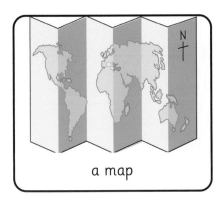

a map

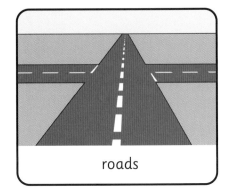

roads

Example

This can help you find a place.   a map

....

Questions

1   This has seven colours. You sometimes see
    it after rain.   ....

2   You can sail boats on this and children like
    swimming in it.   ....

3   You can only see these at night.   ....

4   Buses and cars have to go on these
    between one place and another.   ....

5   It is often cold on top of these.   ....

6   There are a lot of trees and plants in this
    hot, green place.   ....

Part 2
– 6 questions –

Look and read. Write yes or no.

Examples

There are five animals in the picture. .... *yes* ....

There are some rocks in the river. .... *no* ....

Questions

1 The brown cow is looking up at the clouds.

....

2 The man who is fishing is sitting on the ground.

....

3 It's a windy day.

....

4 One of the sheep has grass in its mouth.

....

5 The girl with long hair is riding a horse.

....

6 There are a lot of cars coming to this place.

....

Part 3
– 6 questions –

Read the text and choose the best answer.

Example

Ben:	Would you like to come to the cinema this evening?

Daisy:	(A) OK.
	B I'd love some.
	C You had to go.

Questions

1   **Ben:**   I'd like to see the film 'The Two Friends'.

     Daisy: A   I don't like any of them.

                 B   I don't know that one.

                 C   I don't think about it.

2   **Daisy:**   What's it about?

    Ben: A   A boy and a dolphin.
                       B   It's next to the supermarket.
                       C   All right!

3   **Daisy:**   Is it at the Park Cinema?

    Ben: A   Yes, it did.
                       B   Yes, it can.
                       C   Yes, it is.

4   **Ben:**   There's a bus that stops outside the cinema.

    Daisy: A   They are slower than mine.
                       B   I like walking better.
                       C   A bus is bigger.

5   **Ben:**   Would you like to come to my house after the film?

    Daisy: A   Yes, I do.
                       B   Yes, I like it.
                       C   Yes, I would.

6   **Ben:**   You can have supper with me and my family.

    Daisy: A   Good night!
                       B   So do I!
                       C   Great!

Part 4
– 7 questions –

Read the story. Choose a word from the box. Write the correct word next to numbers 1–6. There is one example.

We are learning about kangaroos at school. Last Tuesday, we .... watched .... a great video about them. After the lesson, I went to the library because I wanted to read more about kangaroos. I found three good **(1)** .... there. I put them in my bag and rode home with them on my bike. At home, my mother gave me a drink and I sat outside on our **(2)** .... to drink it because it was a very **(3)** .... day. I told Mum about my lessons at school and about the library. She **(4)** .... and said, 'They have some new animals at the zoo. Do you want to go and see them?' 'What animals are they?' I asked. 'Well,' she said, 'They eat **(5)** .... from trees, they are brown and they **(6)** .... up and down a lot!'

'Kangaroos!' I laughed.

Example

watched	leaves	sunny
smiled	surprised	books
drove	balcony	jump

(7) Now choose the best name for the story.

Tick one box.

A film about animals ☐

My favourite pet ☐

Something new at the zoo ☐

Part 5
– 10 questions –

Look at the pictures and read the story. Write words to complete the sentences about the story. You can use 1, 2 or 3 words.

Tony's birthday

When Tony was eight, one of his presents was a new scarf. 'It's better than my new comics and computer games,' he thought. It was yellow and blue – his favourite colours. He wore it every day. After four weeks, his father said, 'Tony, your scarf is very dirty now. We must wash it.'

Examples

Tony was .... eight .... on his birthday.

Tony liked his new scarf better than his comics and ..... computer games.

Questions

1   The two colours of Tony's scarf were ....

2   Tony wore his new scarf every ....

3   The scarf was very .... after four weeks.

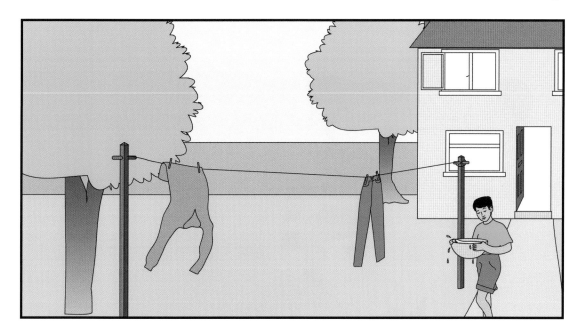

The next morning, before breakfast, Tony washed the scarf carefully in a bowl of water. After breakfast, he put it in the garden because it was wet. Then he went to school.

After school, he went out into the garden to find his scarf.

It was clean again, but the colour was different. It was green and very, very long. Tony didn't like the new colour and when he put the scarf on, it went down to his feet. Tony was sad. He ran inside the house and started to cry.

4   Tony .... before breakfast.

5   Tony put the wet scarf in ....

6   When Tony came home, the colour of the scarf in the garden was
     ....

7   Tony went .... and started to cry.

'What's the matter?' his dad asked. 'Look at my scarf!' Tony said. 'It's green and long. I don't like it now.'

'Oh, Tony,' his dad said. 'That's not your scarf. That's Mum's! Yours is in your bedroom. I took it inside because it started to rain.'

'Thank you, Dad!' Tony said. Then they both laughed and Tony went to play football with his friends.

8   Tony didn't like the scarf because it was green and because it was too

     ....

9   The green scarf was Tony's ....

10   Tony's father put Tony's scarf in his ....

Blank Page

Part 6

– 5 questions –

Read the text. Choose the right words and write them on the lines.

Choosing a pet

Example Choosing the right pet is difficult. You ....*have*.............. to think very carefully!

Dogs   like   being   with   people   and   need   to

1 .... for long walks. They are good pets

2 for people .... live in the countryside.

Cats are happy in towns, but it's good for them to have a

3 garden   to   play   .... run   in.

4 .... people love smaller animals like mice,

snakes or spiders!

5 When you choose a pet, think .... these

questions: What kind of home does it need? What does it like

to eat? And where does it like to play?

Example	have	must	can
1	going	go	went
2	who	which	when
3	and	than	because
4	A	The	Some
5	about	after	above

Part 1
– 5 questions –

Listen and draw lines. There is one example.

Sally   Mary   Jim   Daisy

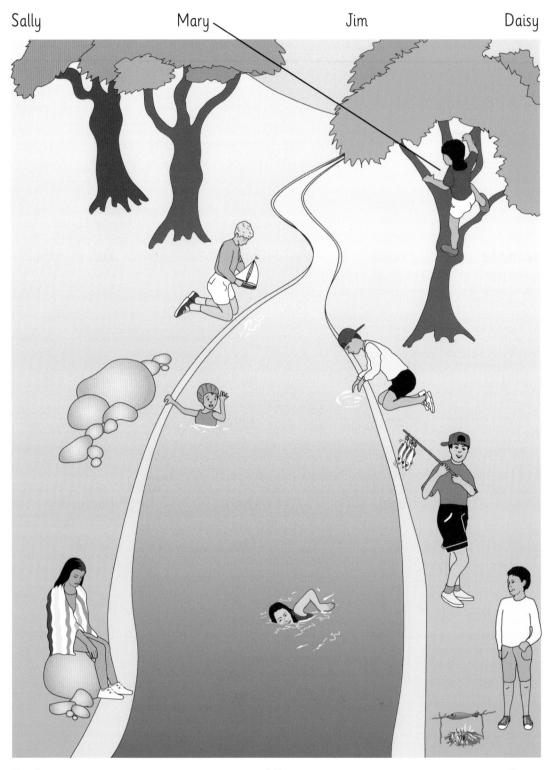

Fred   Jill   Peter

Part 2

– 5 questions –

Listen and write. There is one example.

The Lake Café

Name: .... Ann Tracy ....

1 | Age: ....

2 | Comes to café: at ....

3 | Favourite sandwich: ....

4 | Would like: ....

5 | Came today with: ....

Part 3
– 5 questions –

What did Tony do last week?
Listen and draw a line from the day to the correct picture. There is one example.

Monday

Tuesday

Wednesday

Thursday

Friday

Saturday

Sunday

Part 4
– 5 questions –

Listen and tick (✔) the box. There is one example.

How did John go to his grandparents' house?

A ☐   **B** ✔   **C** ☐

1   What did Jane watch on TV?

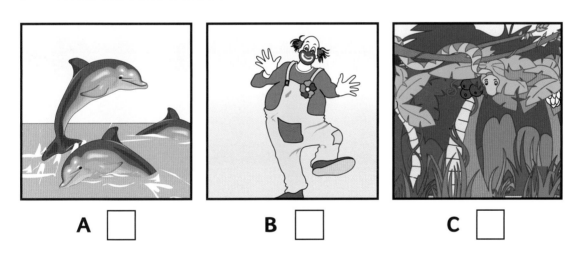

A ☐   **B** ☐   **C** ☐

2   What's the matter with Sue?

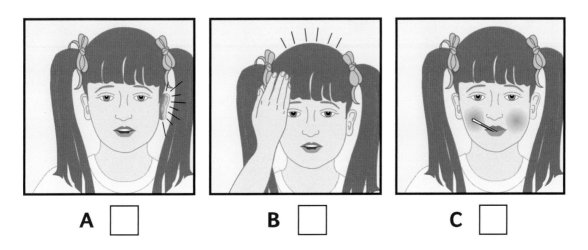

A ☐   **B** ☐   **C** ☐

47

3   What do they need to wash?

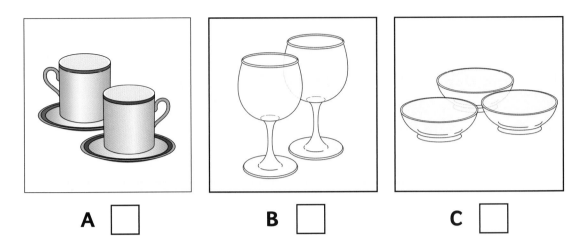

A □   B □   C □

4   Which boy is Ben's brother?

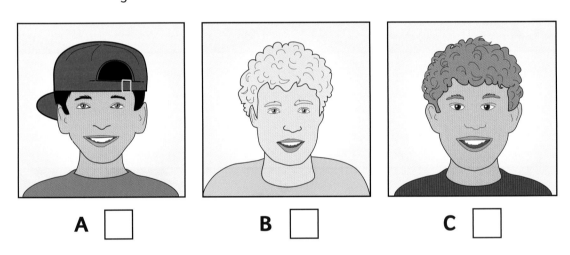

A □   B □   C □

5   What can't Sam find?

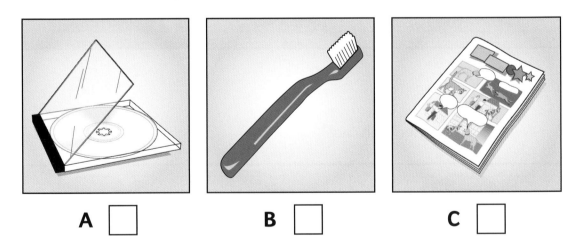

A □   B □   C □

Part 5
– 5 questions –

Listen and colour and draw. There is one example.

Reading and Writing

Part 1

– 6 questions –

Look and read. Choose the correct words and write them on the lines. There is one example.

a scarf

a party

a picnic

tea

music

a film

soup

a coat

Example

You have this outside on a beach or on the
grass.   ....a picnic........

Questions

1   You can listen or dance to this.   ....

2   This is like a jacket, but it is longer.   ....

3   You have this food in a bowl.   ....

4   This is long and you wear it round your neck.   ....

5   This is a drink. Some people have it with milk.   ....

6   You can see this at a cinema or at home on
a video.   ....

Part 2
– 6 questions –

Look and read. Write yes or no.

Examples

There is a clock on the school wall. ....*yes*..........

All the children are outside the school. ....*no*..........

Questions

1   Three girls are skipping.   ....

2   It's a windy day and the leaves are
    flying off the trees.   ....

3   Two boys are climbing up one of
    the trees.   ....

4   A girl is playing on the squares.   ....

5   You can see twenty children in the
    playground.   ....

6   The boy sitting under the tree has
    got curly hair.   ....

Part 3
– 6 questions –

Read the text and choose the best answer.

Example

Nick:	Hi, Tom! Where are you going?

Tom:	(A) I'm going to the park.
	B I go to the park.
	C I went to the park.

Questions

1 **Nick:**   Can I come with you?

   Tom: A   Yes, you do.
              B   Yes, you can.
              C   Yes, you are.

2 **Nick:** Do you like skating?

 Tom: A   Yes, I liked it.
            B   Yes, I'm OK.
            C   Yes, I love it.

3 **Nick:** We can skate in the park. Shall we go there now?

 Tom: A   All right.
            B   It's fine.
            C   We are.

4 **Nick:** Can you skate well?

 Tom: A   Yes, I'm well.
            B   Yes, please.
            C   Yes, it's easy.

5 **Nick:** What sports do you like?

 Tom: A   I like playing football.
            B   I am playing football.
            C   I can play football.

6 **Nick:** I often play football at the beach. Would you like to come with me on Saturday?

 Tom: A   Sorry, I can't.
            B   Sorry, I didn't.
            C   Sorry, I'm not.

 Nick: How about Sunday?

 Tom: Great!

Part 4

– 7 questions –

Read the story. Choose a word from the box. Write the correct word next to numbers 1–6. There is one example.

Fred was an animal that lived in a zoo. Every morning, a man came to Fred's house and ....washed.... him to make him nice and clean. Then he gave Fred **(1)** .... to drink and some food. Sometimes he gave him **(2)** .... to eat. Fred loved bananas and always wanted more! One day, the man didn't **(3)** .... the door well and Fred quietly walked out. The **(4)** .... in the town were very surprised! Fred saw a supermarket and went in. He saw lots of bananas and started eating them. The man in the supermarket **(5)** .... the zoo. 'Your elephant is eating the food in our shop. Please come quickly!' But Fred started walking home to the zoo. When he went back into his house again, he was tired but very **(6)** .... 'I've had an exciting day,' Fred thought.

Example

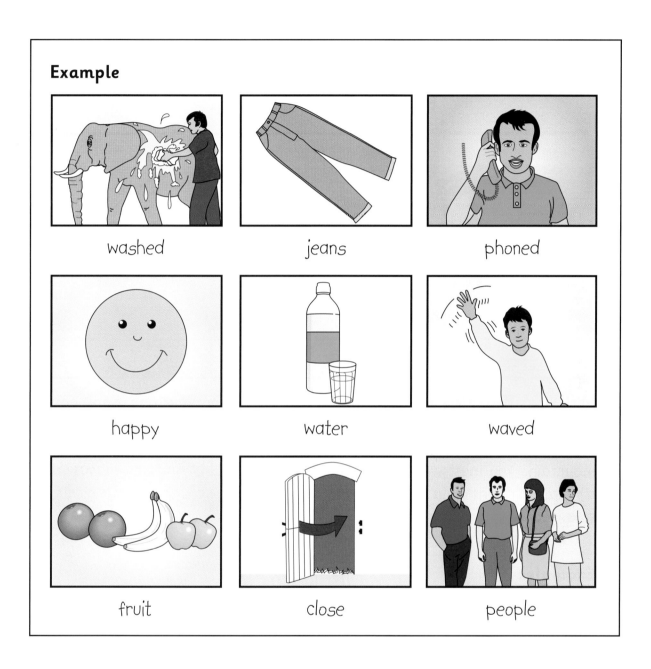

washed

jeans

phoned

happy

water

waved

fruit

close

people

(7) Now choose the best name for the story.

Tick one box.

Fred buys some bananas ☐

Fred goes to town ☐

Fred's holiday at the zoo ☐

Part 5

– 10 questions –

Look at the pictures and read the story. Write words to complete the sentences about the story. You can use 1, 2 or 3 words.

Ben's day in the mountains

My name's Ben. I live in a town with my dad, mum and our dog, Sam. Last holiday, we went to see my grandparents. I love going to see them because they live in the mountains. One day, Dad, Mum and I wanted to climb a mountain. 'You must wear strong shoes,' Grandpa said. 'And you must take a map,' said Grandma and she gave me one. 'And we must take a picnic,' said Dad.

Examples

.... Sam .... is the name of Ben's dog.

Ben went to ......the mountains...... to see his grandparents.

Questions

1   Ben and his parents wanted to .... a mountain.

2   Ben's grandfather wanted them to wear ....

3   Ben's grandmother gave him a .... to take up the mountain.

We started climbing. It was sunny. Sam was very happy. He ran in front of us. It was very beautiful at the top of the mountain. Mum sat on a rock and looked at the map. Dad took some pictures of us.

We had our picnic, then I played in a waterfall and Sam tried to catch rabbits. 'Stop, Sam!' I said. 'You mustn't run after rabbits.'

4 .... looked at the map at the top of the mountain.

5 Ben's father .... of his family.

6 After the picnic, Ben played in a ....

7 Sam ran after some ....

When we started walking down the mountain, Dad said, 'Look at those black clouds!' It started raining.

'I can't see,' I said. I was afraid. 'It's OK,' said Dad. 'We've got Sam with us. He can help us.' Dad was right. Sam walked in front of us and found my grandparents' house again.

We had a hot dinner and I gave Sam his favourite food. 'Thank you, Sam,' I said. 'You're a very good dog.'

8   Ben was .... because he couldn't see well.

9   Sam found Ben's .... again.

10   Ben gave Sam some of his .... because he was a good dog.

Blank Page

Part 6
– 5 questions –

Read the text. Choose the right words and write them on the lines.

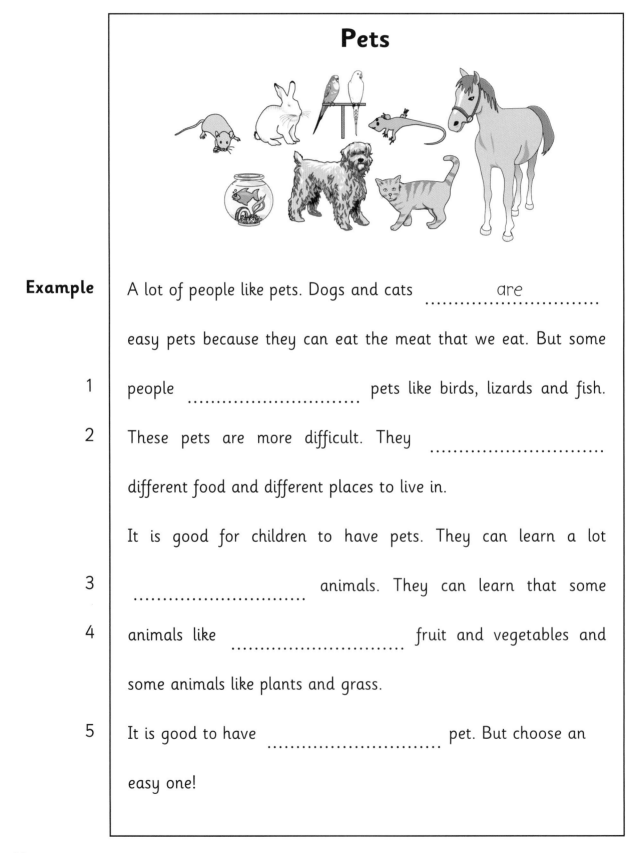

Pets

Example	A lot of people like pets. Dogs and cats ....*are*.............. easy pets because they can eat the meat that we eat. But some
1	people .... pets like birds, lizards and fish.
2	These pets are more difficult. They .... different food and different places to live in.
	It is good for children to have pets. They can learn a lot
3	.... animals. They can learn that some
4	animals like .... fruit and vegetables and some animals like plants and grass.
5	It is good to have .... pet. But choose an easy one!

Example	is	were	are
1	has	have	had
2	need	needs	needing
3	about	of	in
4	ate	eats	eating
5	an	some	a

Blank Page

Speaking

Find the difference

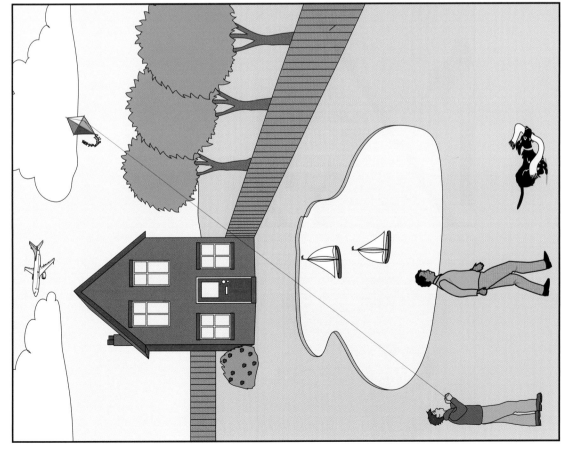

Story

Find the different ones

Blank Page

Find the difference

Story

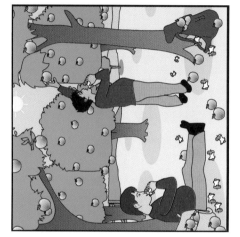

Find the different ones

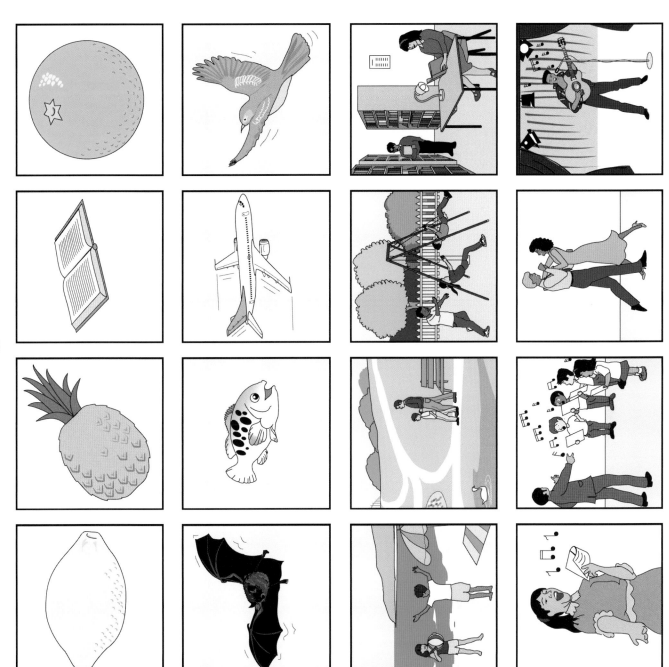

71

Blank Page

Speaking

Find the difference

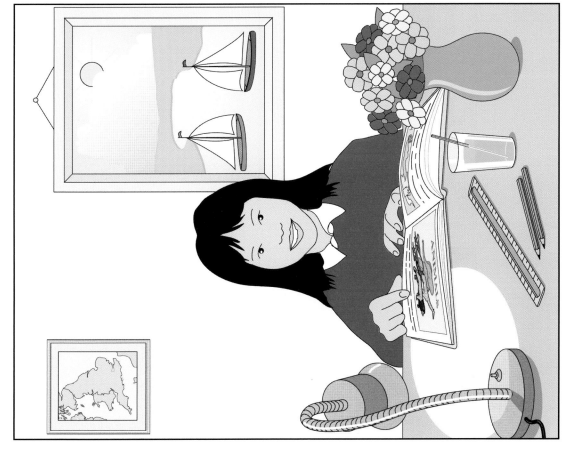

Story

Find the different ones

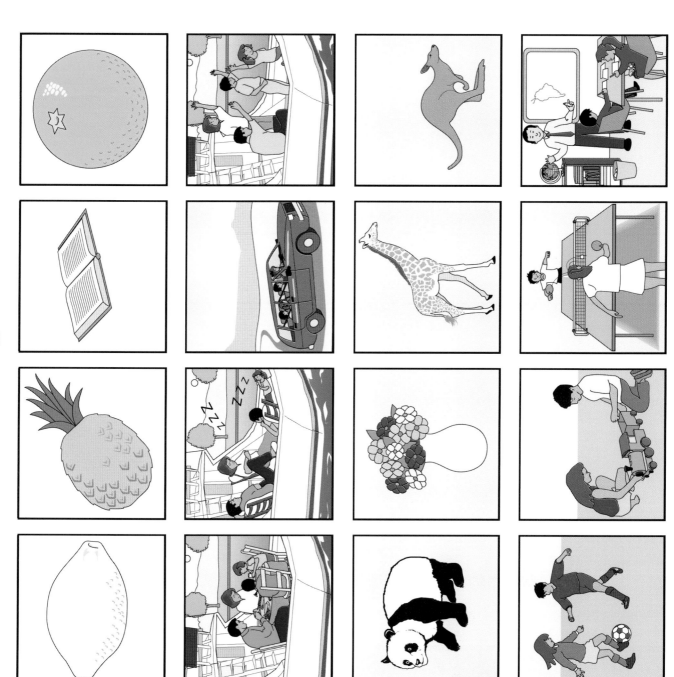